Dreamadillo

For:

By Tina Marie Bevan

For Derek, who's always believed in this dream of mine... I love you!
And for all my cherished family and friends who helped me along the way... Thank you! TMB

"Armadillo sleeps on the dry desert sand...
But his mind soars high above the land.
As he sheds the shell he needs to hide in,
He grows dream wings with which to guide him!

Dreamadillo is now in the clouds...
His bubble wand at rest.
He looks into his pocket for
Your special dream request.

He dips his wand into the jar...
And as you close your eyes,
Dream bubbles float on down to you
Across the moonlit skies..."

Printed in South Korea
Story and illustrations by Tina Marie Bevan
Copyright 2015

ISBN 978-0-9908532-0-6

Like this sleeping armadillo,
it's always a surprise
where your dreams will take you
when you close your eyes...

Dreamadillo, Dreamadillo... Send a good dream down to my pillow!

Up on a cloud in his traveling home, lives Dreamadillo, no desert to roam.

His job is to keep all the nightmares away... from slumbering children, so GOOD dreams can play!

All through the night, you will dream more and more, of unicorns, rainbows and candy galore.

Whatever your Dream Wish happens to be...   Dreamadillo will help you. Just wait and see!

Do you see all the happy dreams? Watch how they float... dreams of flying, and riding, or sailing a boat!

His magical Bubble Wand sends them on down... the RIGHT dreams delivered to each kid in town!

With his Dream Gadget, Dreamadillo will trap pesky nightmares away in just a quick snap!

He'll jar up those bad dreams and lock them up tight, so you'll have a wonderful, sweet dreamy night!

Dreamadillo enjoys saving dreams of each kind, after you dream them, he hopes you won't mind!

He'll tag them and keep them inside his Dream Jars. The collection is kept way up high, near the stars!

Then out of the blue, there comes a surprise! Who dares to steal dreams right in front of our eyes?

It's Buttons the Buzzard and Tricky the Snake! Those bandits are looking for good dreams to take!

Because they want pleasant dreams all to themselves, they go around stealing Dream Jars from the shelves!

It might be because way back in the nest, they were told they could never be more than a pest!

So they bumble and tumble, they zip and they zoom! Is it nice to steal dreams from a little kid's room?

Why in the world do they cause so much trouble? Is it right to steal anyone's special Dream Bubble?

"You can't steal MY dreams!" Speak up and be heard... You TELL that mean snake and that silly old bird!

BAD DREAMS!

Then into the night, Dreamadillo will soar! Those pests aren't allowed to bug YOU anymore!

Dream bandits are sneaky and might try to steal... your very BEST dreams, the ones that are REAL!

Dreamadillo has something he'll now share with you... YOU have the power to make dreams come true!

Our Dreams are Colorful!

Have confidence and your dreams will take flight, with practice, and patience, and just enough might...

Like Dreamadillo, you'll sprout wings and soar... reaching new heights like never before!

Dreamadillo believes that you'll find the way... to live out your dreams with every new day.

What's your Dream Wish?

No matter if pests try to get in your way... your dreams are kept safe. In your heart, they will stay.

When you're all tucked in bed, cuddled up nice and tight, and it's just about time to turn off your light...

Snuggle up in your blanket and hug your soft pillow. You'll have the BEST dreams with your pal, Dreamadillo!

For more fun and adventures with Dreamadillo,
please visit www.Dreamadillo.com.